The Little Frenchman And His Water Lots

GEORGE POPE MORRIS

[ZHINGOORA BOOKS]

THE LITTLE FRENCHMAN AND HIS WATER LOTS

Look into those they call unfortunate,
And, closer view'd, you'll find they are
unwise.—*Young.*

Let wealth come in by comely thrift,
And not by any foolish shift:

Tis haste makes waste:
Who gripes too hard the dry and slippery
sand
Holds none at all, or little, in his hand.—
Herrick.

Let well alone.—*Proverb.*

How much real comfort every one might enjoy if he would be contented with the lot in which heaven has cast him, and how much trouble would be avoided if people would only "let well alone." A moderate independence, quietly and honestly procured, is certainly every way preferable even to immense possessions achieved by the wear and tear of mind and body so necessary to procure them. Yet there are very few individuals, let them be doing ever so well in the world, who are not always straining every nerve to do better; and this is one of the many causes why failures in business so frequently occur among us. The present generation seem unwilling to "realize" by slow and sure degrees; but choose rather to set their whole hopes upon a single cast, which either makes or mars them forever!

Gentle reader, do you remember Monsieur Poopoo? He used to keep a small toy-store in Chatham, near the corner of Pearl Street. You must recollect him, of course. He lived there for many years, and was one of the most polite and accommodating of shopkeepers. When a juvenile, you have bought tops and marbles of him a thousand times. To be sure you have; and seen his vinegar-visage lighted up with a smile as you flung him the coppers; and you have laughed at his little straight queue and his dimity breeches, and all the other oddities that made up the every-day apparel of my little Frenchman. Ah, I perceive you recollect him now.

Well, then, there lived Monsieur Poopoo ever since he came from "dear, delightful Paris," as he was wont to call the city of his nativity—there he took in the pennies for his kickshaws—there he laid aside five thousand dollars against a rainy day—there he was as happy as a lark—and there, in all human probability, he would have been to this very day, a respected and substantial citizen, had he been willing to "let well alone." But Monsieur Poopoo had heard strange stories about the prodigious rise in real estate; and, having understood that most of his neighbors had become suddenly rich by speculating in lots, he instantly grew dissatisfied with his own lot, forthwith determined to shut up shop, turn everything into cash, and set about making money in right-down earnest. No sooner said than done; and our quondam storekeeper a few days afterward attended an extensive sale of real estate, at the Merchants' Exchange.

There was the auctioneer, with his beautiful and inviting lithographic maps—all the lots as smooth and square and enticingly laid out as possible—and there were the speculators—and there, in the midst of them, stood Monsieur Poopoo.

"Here they are, gentlemen," said he of the hammer, "the most valuable lots ever offered for sale. Give me a bid for them!"

"One hundred each," said a bystander.

"One hundred!" said the auctioneer, "scarcely enough to pay for the maps. One hundred—going—and fifty—gone! Mr. H., they are yours. A noble purchase. You'll sell those same lots in less than a fortnight for fifty thousand dollars profit!"

Monsieur Poopoo pricked up his ears at this, and was lost in astonishment. This was a much easier way certainly of accumulating riches than selling toys in Chatham Street, and he determined to buy and mend his fortune without delay.

The auctioneer proceeded in his sale. Other parcels were offered and disposed of, and all the purchasers were promised immense advantages for their enterprise. At last came a more valuable parcel than all the rest. The company pressed around the stand, and Monsieur Poopoo did the same.

"I now offer you, gentlemen, these magnificent lots, delightfully situated on Long Island, with valuable water privileges. Property in fee—title indisputable—terms of sale, cash—deeds ready for delivery immediately after the sale. How much for them? Give them a start at something. How much?" The auctioneer looked around; there were no bidders. At last he caught the eye of Monsieur Poopoo. "Did you say one hundred, sir? Beautiful lots— valuable water privileges—shall I say one hundred for you?"

"*Oui, monsieur*; I will give you von hundred dollar apiece, for de lot vid de valuarble vatare privalege; *c'est ça.*"

"Only one hundred apiece for these sixty valuable lots—only one hundred—going—going— going—gone!"

Monsieur Poopoo was the fortunate possessor. The auctioneer congratulated him— the sale closed—and the company dispersed.

"*Pardonnez-moi, monsieur*," said Poopoo, as the auctioneer descended his pedestal, "you shall *excusez-moi*, if I shall go to *votre bureau*, your counting-house, ver quick to make every ting sure wid respec to de lot vid de valuarble vatare privalege. Von leetle bird in de hand he vorth two in de tree, *c'est vrai—* eh?"

"Certainly, sir."

"Vell den, *allons*."

And the gentlemen repaired to the counting-house, where the six thousand dollars were paid, and the deeds of the property delivered. Monsieur Poopoo put these carefully in his pocket, and as he was about taking his leave, the auctioneer made him a present of the lithographic outline of the lots, which was a very liberal thing on his part, considering the map was a beautiful specimen of that glorious art. Poopoo could not admire it sufficiently. There were his sixty lots, as uniform as possible, and his little gray eyes sparkled like diamonds as they wandered from one end of the spacious sheet to the other.

Poopoo's heart was as light as a feather, and he snapped his fingers in the very wantonness of joy as he repaired to Delmonico's, and ordered the first good French dinner that had gladdened his palate since his arrival in America.

After having discussed his repast, and washed it down with a bottle of choice old claret, he resolved upon a visit to Long Island to view his purchase. He consequently immediately hired a horse and gig, crossed the

Brooklyn ferry, and drove along the margin of the river to the Wallabout, the location in question.

Our friend, however, was not a little perplexed to find his property. Everything on the map was as fair and even as possible, while all the grounds about him were as undulated as they could well be imagined, and there was an elbow of the East River thrusting itself quite into the ribs of the land, which seemed to have no business there. This puzzled the Frenchman exceedingly; and, being a stranger in those parts, he called to a farmer in an adjacent field.

"*Mon ami*, are you acquaint vid dis part of de country—eh?"

"Yes, I was born here, and know every inch of it."

"Ah, *c'est bien*, dat vill do," and the Frenchman got out of the gig, tied the horse, and produced his lithographic map.

"Den maybe you vill have de kindness to show me de sixty lot vich I have bought, vid de valuarble vatare privalege?"

The farmer glanced his eye over the paper.

"Yes, sir, with pleasure; if you will be good enough to *get into my boat, I will row you out to them*!"

"Vat dat you say, sure?"

"My friend," said the farmer, "this section of Long Island has recently been bought up by the speculators of New York, and laid out for a great city; but the principal street is only visible *at low tide*. When this part of the East River is filled up, it will be just there. Your lots, as you will perceive, are beyond it; *and are now all under water*."

At first the Frenchman was incredulous. He could not believe his senses. As the facts, however, gradually broke upon him, he shut one eye, squinted obliquely at the heavens—-the river—the farmer—and then he turned away and squinted at them all over again! There was his purchase sure enough; but then it could not be perceived for there was a river flowing over it! He drew a box from his waistcoat pocket, opened it, with an emphatic knock upon the lid, took a pinch of snuff and restored it to his waistcoat pocket as before. Poopoo was evidently in trouble, having "thoughts which often lie too deep for tears"; and, as his grief was also too big for words, he untied his horse, jumped into his gig, and returned to the auctioneer in hot haste.

It was near night when he arrived at the auction-room—his horse in a foam and himself in a fury. The auctioneer was leaning back in his chair, with his legs stuck out of a low window, quietly smoking a cigar after the labors of the day, and humming the music from the last new opera.

"Monsieur, I have much plaisir to fin' you, *chez vous*, at home."

"Ah, Poopoo! glad to see you. Take a seat, old boy."

"But I shall not take de seat, sare."

"No—why, what's the matter?"

"Oh, *beaucoup* de matter. I have been to see de gran lot vot you sell me to-day."

"Well, sir, I hope you like your purchase?"

"No, monsieur, I no like him."

"I'm sorry for it; but there is no ground for your complaint."

"No, sare; dare is no *ground* at all—de ground is all vatare!"

"You joke!"

"I no joke. I nevare joke; *je n'entends pas la raillerie*, Sare, *voulez-vous* have de kindness to give me back de money vot I pay!"

"Certainly not."

"Den vill you be so good as to take de East River off de top of my lot?"

"That's your business, sir, not mine."

"Den I make von *mauvaise affaire*—von gran mistake!"

"I hope not. I don't think you have thrown your money away in the *land*."

"No, sare; but I tro it avay in de *vatare!*"

"That's not my fault."

"Yes, sare, but it is your fault. You're von ver gran rascal to swindle me out of *de l'argent*."

"Hello, old Poopoo, you grow personal; and if you can't keep a civil tongue in your head, you must go out of my counting-room."

"Vare shall I go to, eh?"

"To the devil, for aught I care, you foolish old Frenchman!" said the auctioneer, waxing warm.

"But, sare, I vill not go to de devil to oblige you!" replied the Frenchman, waxing warmer. "You sheat me out of all de dollar vot I make in Shatham Street; but I vill not go to de devil for all dat. I vish you may go to de devil yourself you dem yankee-doo-dell, and I vill go and drown myself, *tout de suite*, right avay."

"You couldn't make a better use of your water privileges, old boy!"

"Ah, *miséricorde!* Ah, *mon dieu, je suis abîmé.* I am ruin! I am done up! I am break all into ten sousan leetle pieces! I am von lame duck, and I shall vaddle across de gran ocean for Paris, vish is de only valuarble vatare privalege dat is left me *à present!*"

Poor Poopoo was as good as his word. He sailed in the next packet, and arrived in Paris almost as penniless as the day he left it.

Should any one feel disposed to doubt the veritable circumstances here recorded, let him cross the East River to the Wallabout, and farmer J—— will *row him out* to the very place where the poor Frenchman's lots still remain *under water*.

End of the book.

www.ingramcontent.com/pod-product-compliance
Lightning Source LLC
Chambersburg PA
CBHW070123010626
45794CB00012B/1254